Zero makes me hungry Zero makes me hungry

Zero makes me hungry Zero makes me hungry

Zero makes me hungry Zero makes me hungry

Zero makes me hungry Zero makes me hungry

Zero makes me hungry Zero makes me hungry

Zero makes me hungry Zero makes me hungry

Zero makes me hungry Zero makes me hungry

Zero makes me hungry Zero makes me hungry

Zero makes me hungry Zero makes me hungry

Zero makes me hungry Zero makes me hungry

Zero makes me hungry Zero makes me hungry

Zero makes me hungry Zero makes me hungry

Zero makes me hungry Zero makes me hungry

zero makes me hungry

a collection of poems for today

Compiled by **Edward Lueders** and **Primus St. John**

Art and Design **John Reuter-Pacyna**

Lothrop, Lee & Shepard Company
A Division of William Morrow & Company, Inc. New York

Trade edition first published 1976

Copyright © 1976 by Scott, Foresman and Company

All rights reserved. No part of this book may be
reproduced or utilized in any form or by any means,
electronic or mechanical, including photocopying,
recording or by any information storage and retrieval
system, without permission in writing from the
Publisher. Inquiries should be addressed to Lothrop,
Lee & Shepard Company, 105 Madison Avenue, New York,
N.Y. 10016

Printed in the United States of America

1 2 3 4 5 80 79 78 77 76

Library of Congress Catalog Card Number 75-33543

ISBN 0-688-41745-0
ISBN 0-688-51745-5

Acknowledgments

Title: "Zero makes me hungry" from the poem "Numbers." Reprinted with permission of Macmillan Publishing Co., Inc. from THE REAL TIN FLOWER by Aliki Barnstone. Copyright © 1968 by Aliki Barnstone.

"The Act." William Carlos Williams, COLLECTED LATER POEMS. Copyright 1948 by William Carlos Williams. Reprinted by permission of New Directions Publishing Corporation. "After Supper" by Hugh McNamar. Reprinted by permission of the author. "Alarm Clock." From FINDING A POEM by Eve Merriam. Copyright © 1970 by Eve Merriam. Used by permission of Atheneum Publishers and Eve Merriam c/o International Creative Management. "Ancestors" by Grey Cohoe. From THE WHISPERING WIND, Terry Allen, Editor. Copyright 1972. Doubleday and Company. Used by permission of the author. "And They Lived Happily Ever After for a While." from FAST AND SLOW by John Ciardi. Copyright © 1975 by John Ciardi. Reprinted by permission of Houghton Mifflin Company. "The Artist." William Carlos Williams, PICTURES FROM BRUEGHEL AND OTHER POEMS. Copyright 1954 by William Carlos Williams. Reprinted by permission of New Directions Publishing Corporation. "At Grandmother's" by John Haislip from NOT EVERY YEAR. Copyright © 1971 by the University of Washington Press. Reprinted by permission. "At quitting time . . ." from BUNCH GRASS, by Robert Sund. Copyright © 1969 by Robert Sund. Reprinted by permission of University of Washington Press.

"Back Yard, July Night." From A BOOK OF NATURE POEMS, edited by William Cole. Copyright © 1969 by William Cole. Reprinted by permission of The Viking Press, Inc. "Battle Won Is Lost" by Philip George from NATIVE AMERICAN ARTS #1, published by the Institute of American Indian Arts. Reprinted by permission of the author. "Breaklight." From AN ORDINARY WOMAN, by Lucille Clifton. Copyright © 1974 by Lucille Clifton. Reprinted by permission of Random House, Inc., and Curtis Brown, Ltd.

"The Cat." From SLEEK FOR THE LONG FLIGHT, by William Matthews. Copyright © 1971, 1972 by William Matthews. Reprinted by permission of Random House, Inc. "The Chinese Greengrocers" by Pat Lowther from THE FIDDLEHEAD, January-February 1970. Reprinted by permission of the author. "Constellations" by Primus St. John. Reprinted by permission of the author.

"The Day We Die" by anonymous (the Kalahari Bushmen), from THE REBIRTH OF THE OSTRICH by Arthur Markowitz. Copyright 1971 by Arthur Markowitz. Reprinted by permission of the publishers, Campbell Museum, Gaborone, Botswana. "Days" from THE WHITSUN WEDDINGS by Philip Larkin. Copyright © 1960, 1961, 1962, 1964, by Philip Larkin. Reprinted by permission of Faber and Faber Ltd. "Don Larsen's Perfect Game." Copyright © 1967 by Paul Goodman. Reprinted from COLLECTED POEMS, by Paul Goodman, edited by Taylor Stoehr, by permission of Random House, Inc. "Done With." From THE DESCENT by Ann Stanford. Copyright © 1970 by Ann Stanford. Reprinted by permission of The Viking Press, Inc. "Don't Tell Anybody." Reprinted from COMPLETE POETRY OF OSIP EMILEVICH MANDELSTAM, translated by Burton Raffel and Alla Burago, by permission of the State University of New York Press, Burton Raffel and Alla Burago. Copyright © 1973 by State University of New York Press. "Drawing by Ronnie C., Grade One" by Ruth Lechlitner, is reprinted from A CHANGING SEASON, by Ruth Lechlitner, copyright 1973, by Branden Press, Inc. Reprinted by permission of Branden Press, Inc. and Ruth Lechlitner. "The Driver" by Joel Lueders from THE SATORIAN, 1970. Reprinted by permission of the author. "The Duck" from VERSES FROM 1929 ON by Ogden Nash (British title: FAMILY REUNION). Copyright, 1931, 1933, 1935, 1936, 1937, 1938, 1939, 1940, 1945, by Ogden Nash. Reprinted by permission of Little, Brown and Co. and J.M. Dent & Sons Ltd.

Table of Contents

A Project for Freight Trains

Sitting at crossings and waiting for freights to pass, we have all noticed words—COTTON BELT / ERIE / BE SPECIFIC—SAY UNION PACIFIC / SOUTHERN SERVES THE SOUTH—going by. I propose to capitalize on this fact in the following way:

All freight cars that have high solid sides—boxcars, refrigerator cars, tank cars, hopper cars, cement cars —should be painted one of eight attractive colors, and have one large word printed on them:

1. Burnt orange freight cars with the word CLOUD in olive drab.
2. Peagreen freight cars with the word STAR in charcoal gray.
3. Rose-red freight cars with the word MEADOW in salmon pink.
4. Glossy black freight cars with the word STEAM in gold.
5. Peach-colored freight cars with the word AIR in royal blue.
6. Peach-colored freight cars with the word PORT in forest green.
7. Lavender freight cars with the word GRASS in vermillion or scarlet.
8. Swiss blue freight cars with the word RISING in chocolate brown.

When this has been accomplished, freight cars should continue to be used in the usual ways, so that the word and color combinations will be entirely random, and unpredictable poems will roll across the landscape.

Freight cars without words (i.e., without high or solid sides, such as flatcars, cattle cars, gondolas, automobile transporters, etc.) should all be painted white, to emphasize their function as spaces in the poems. Cabooses can be this color too, with a large black dot, the only punctuation.

Approximations of these random train poems can be arrived at by using the numbers above, plus 9 and 0 for spaces, and combining serial numbers from dollar bills, social security numbers, birthdates, and telephone numbers. The 5-6 combination, which makes AIRPORT, is to be considered a lucky omen. 2-6 may be even luckier.

This project would need to be carried out over the entire United States at once. Every five years a competition could be held among poets to see who can provide the best set of colors and words for the next time.

David Young

Progress

There are two ways now
To cross the mountain.

One is a foot-path;
My father walked it beside his *burro*,
The *burro* loaded with eggs in boxes
To trade for *chile* and plums and apples
    In Chimayó.

One is a highway;
Your automobile, I watch it climbing
In such a hurry, on easy curvings
That slide beneath you and wave behind you—
    Pronto! You pass!

The path takes longer;
A week in going, a week in coming;
A man can see more, hear more, and feel more,
Learn more of the wisdom in long, slow thinking
    Along the trail.

But, as *senõr* says,
We have the highway. All the old wisdom
Does not much matter. If I could buy me
An automobile, I would not trade it
    For any *burro!*

Edith Agnew

Pony Song

i do not ride a painted pony
i've never felt his strong lean stride
    i ride a car from detroit
        and i sit in class
where they teach me about the great
                    white
                    romans
and not of my dry brown mother
the painted ponies have all gone
        only my grandmother remembers
    i ride a car from detroit
and my dry brown earth-mother
      will not speak to me now.

Rudy Bantista

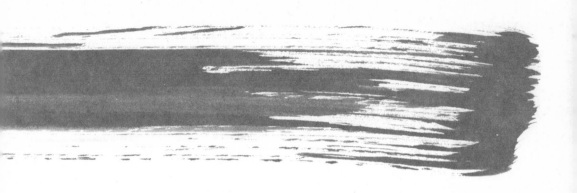

Learning About the Indians

He danced in feathers, with paint across his nose.
Thump, thump went the drum, and bumped our blood,
And sent a strange vibration through the mind.
White Eagle, he was called, or Mr. White,

And he strutted for money now, in schoolrooms built
On Ohio's plains, surrounded by the graves
Of all of our fathers, but more of his than ours.
Our teachers called it Extracurricular.

We called it fun. And as for Mr. White,
Changed back to a shabby salesman's suit, he called it
Nothing at all as he packed his drums, and drove,
Tires screeching, out of the schoolyard into the night.

Mary Oliver

NEEDS

I want something suited to my special needs
I want chrome hubcaps, pin-on attachments
and year round use year after year
I want a workhorse with smooth uniform cut,
dozer blade and snow blade & deluxe steering
wheel
I want something to mow, throw snow, tow, and sow with
I want precision reel blades
I want a console-styled dashboard
I want an easy spintype recoil starter
I want combination bevel and spur gears, 14
gauge stamped steel housing and
washable foam element air cleaner
I want a pivoting front axle and extrawide turf tires
I want an inch of foam rubber inside a vinyl
covering
and especially if it's not too much, if I
can deserve it, even if I can't pay for it
I want to mow while riding

A. R. Ammons

THROUGH
THE AUTOMATIC CARWASH

Through the automatic carwash,
windows closed, water zinging
on metal, the windshield fogging,
the moving tread gives us
the idea of moving through a summer
thundershower in Missouri
at ten miles an hour,
windshield fogging,
hailstones banging on the hood,
darkness settling on us—and
the giant rollerbrushes thundering
down make my son say
I don't like this, and I
switch on the overhead light.

Robert Vas Dias

The Owl on the Aerial

Just at dusk
As the full moon rose
And filled his canyon,
Out of his crevice
Floated the owl,
His down-edged wings
Silent as moonlight.

With three-foot wingspread,
Claws that could paralyze
Rabbit or squirrel,
He battened on beetles
Drawn to the manlight,
And just for a little
He lit on the aerial,
His curved claws clutching
The shining metal.

Softly the moonlight
Sheened on his feathers
While under his feet,
Unfelt by him,
The moon lay still
And men like those
In the house below
Floated upon it.

Clarice Short

THE TELEVISION

Unaccustomed
to movement
and real life
it crept
to the window
and,
delicately
lifting the blind
with a long
aluminum
tentacle,
sat
looking out
at the night.

Geoffrey Godbey

JETLINER

now he takes his mark
at the very farthest end of the runway
looking straight ahead, eager, intense
with his sharp eyes shining

he takes a deep, deep breath
with his powerful lungs
expanding his massive chest
his burning heart beating like thunders

then . . . after a few . . . tense moments . . . of pondering
he roars at his utmost
and slowly begins to jog
kicking the dark earth hard
and now he begins to run
kicking the dark earth harder
then he dashes, dashes like mad, like mad
howling, shouting, screaming, and roaring

then with a most violent kick
he shakes off the earth's pull
softly lifting himself into the air
soaring higher and higher and higher still
piercing the sea of clouds
up into the chandelier of stars

                                    Naoshi Koriyama

BACK YARD, JULY NIGHT

Firefly, airplane, satellite, star—
How I wonder which you are.

William Cole

And They Lived Happily Ever After for a While

John Ciardi

It was down by the Dirty River
  As the Smog was beginning to thin
Because we had been so busy
  Breathing the worst of it in,

That the worst remained inside us
  And whatever we breathed back
Was only—sort of—grayish,
  Or at least not entirely black.

It was down by the Dirty River
  That flows to the Sticky Sea
I gave my heart to my Bonnie,
  And she gave hers to me.

I coughed: "I love you, Bonnie
  And do you love me true?"
The tears of joy flowed from my eyes
  When she sneezed back: "Yes—Achoo!"

It was high in the Garbage Mountains,
  In Saint Snivens by the Scent,
I married my darling Bonnie
  And we built our Oxygen Tent.

And here till the tanks are empty
  We sit and watch TV
And dream of the Dirty River
  On its way to the Sticky Sea.

Here till the needles quiver
  Shut on the zero mark
We sit hand in hand while the TV screen
  Shines like a moon in the dark.

I cough: "I love you, Bonnie.
  And do you love me true?"
And tears of joy flow from our eyes
  When she sneezes: "Yes—Achoo!"

MAN IN ORBIT

* * * * * *

*While*freighting*f
rom*Earth*to*Venus*we
*passed*a*man*without*a
*spacesuit.*He*was*not*pleasant
*to*look*at,*orbiting*the*Sun.
*And*I*remembered*how*he*w
ould*repeat*a*modish*phrase*ba
ck*on*Earth,*endlessly—*Stop*
the*world,*I*want*to*get
*off.*And*it*appeared*t
hat**someone*had.*

* * * * * *

D. O. Pitches

For Poets

Stay beautiful
but don't stay down underground too long
Don't turn into a mole
or a worm
or a root
or a stone

Come on out into the sunlight
Breathe in trees
Knock out mountains
Commune with snakes
& be the very hero of birds

Don't forget to poke your head up
& blink
Think
Walk all around
Swim upstream

Don't forget to fly

Al Young

Don't Tell Anybody

Don't tell anybody,
forget everything you saw—
a bird, an old woman, a jail,
anything. . .

Or else, the minute you unlock
your lips, when dawn comes
you'll start to shake
like a fine-firred pine tree.

And you'll remember a wasp at the summer cottage,
a children's pencil-case,
or forest blueberries
you never picked.

Osip Emilevich Mandelstam

Translated by Burton Raffel
and Alla Burago

THE SECRET

Two girls discover
the secret of life
in a sudden line of
poetry.

I who don't know the
secret wrote
the line. They
told me

(through a third person)
they had found it
but not what it was
not even

what line it was. No doubt
by now, more than a week
later, they have forgotten
the secret,

the line, the name of
the poem. I love them
for finding what
I can't find,

and for loving me
for the line I wrote,
and for forgetting it
so that

a thousand times, till death
finds them, they may
discover it again, in other
lines

in other
happenings. And for
wanting to know it,
for

assuming there is
such a secret, yes,
for that
most of all.

Denise Levertov

31

THE UNWRITTEN

Inside this pencil
crouch words that have never been written
never been spoken
never been thought

they're hiding

they're awake in there
dark in the dark
hearing us
but they won't come out
not for love not for time not for fire

even when the dark has worn away
they'll still be there
hiding in the air
multitudes in days to come may walk through them
breathe them
be none the wiser

what script can it be
that they won't unroll
in what language
would I recognize it
would I be able to follow it
to make out the real names
of everything

maybe there aren't
many
it could be that there's only one word
and it's all we need
it's here in this pencil

every pencil in the world
is like this

W. S. Merwin

Tartars, Uzbeks, Samoyeds

Tartars, Uzbeks, Samoyeds,
all the Ukrainians,
even the Volga Germans
are waiting for their translators.

And maybe this very minute
some Japanese is translating
me into Turkish
and has reached the depths of my soul.

Osip Emilevich Mandelstam

Translated by Burton Raffel
and Alla Burago

POEM:
A REMINDER

Capital letters prompting every line,
Lines printed down the center of each page,
Clear spaces between groups of these, combine
In a convention of respectable age
To mean: "Read carefully. Each word we chose
Has rhythm and sound and sense. This is not prose."

Robert Graves

Winter Poem

once a snowflake fell
on my brow and i loved
it so much and i kissed
it and it was happy and called its cousins
and brothers and a web
of snow engulfed me then
i reached to love them all
and i squeezed them and they became
a spring rain and i stood perfectly
still and was a flower

Nikki Giovanni

White Butterfly

What wisdom do you offer me,
Little white butterfly?
You open your wordless pages, and
Close again your wordless pages.

In your opened pages:
Solitude;
In your closed pages:
Solitude.

Tai Wang-Shu

Translated by Kai-yu Hsu

Drawing
by Ronnie C., Grade One

For the sky, blue. But the six-year-
old searching his crayon-box, finds
no blue to match that sky
framed by the window—a see-through shine
over treetops, housetops. The wax colors
hold only dead light, not this waterflash
thinning to silver
at morning's far edge.
Gray won't do, either:
gray is for rain that you make with
dark slanting lines down-paper.

                              Try orange!

—Draw a larger corner circle for sun, egg-yolk solid,
with yellow strokes leaping outward
like fire bloom—a brightness shouting
flower-shape wind shape joy shape!

The boy sighs, with leg-twisting bliss creating. . .

It is done. The stubby crayons
(all ten of them) are stuffed back
bumpily into their box.

Ruth Lechlitner

MAGIC WORDS

In the very earliest time,
when both people and animals lived on earth,
a person could become an animal if he wanted to
and an animal could become a human being.
Sometimes they were people
and sometimes animals
and there was no difference.
All spoke the same language.
That was the time when words were like magic.
The human mind had mysterious powers.
A word spoken by chance
might have strange consequences.
It would suddenly come alive
and what people wanted to happen could happen.
Nobody could explain this:
That's the way it was.

Netsilik origin (Eskimo)

Translated by Edward Field

DAYS

What are days for?
Days are where we live.
They come, they wake us
Time and time over.
They are to be happy in:
Where can we live but days?

Ah, solving that question
Brings the priest and the doctor
In their long coats
Running over the fields.

Philip Larkin

DON LARSEN'S PERFECT GAME

Everybody went to bat three times
except their pitcher (twice) and his pinch hitter,
but nobody got anything at all.
Don Larsen in the eighth and ninth looked pale
and afterwards he did not want to talk.
This is a fellow who will have bad dreams.
His catcher Berra jumped for joy and hugged him
like a bear, legs and arms, and all the Yankees
crowded around him thick to make him be
not lonely, and in fact in fact in fact
nothing went wrong. But that was yesterday.

Paul Goodman

The Act

There were the roses, in the rain.
Don't cut them, I pleaded.
      They won't last, she said
But they're so beautiful
      where they are.
Agh, we were all beautiful once, she
      said,
and cut them and gave them to me
      in my hand.

William Carlos Williams

SEVENTY-SIX

A man is born gentle and weak.
At his death he is hard and stiff.
Green plants are tender and filled with sap.
At their death they are withered and dry.

Therefore the stiff and unbending is the disciple of death.
The gentle and yielding is the disciple of life.

Thus an army without flexibility never wins a battle.
A tree that is unbending is easily broken.

The hard and strong will fall.
The soft and weak will overcome.

Lao Tsu

Translated by Gia-fu Feng
and Jane English

At Grandmother's

She lay in bed on the second floor,
Dying in quiet that whole season—
While I played catch behind the barn
Each afternoon,
And bounced the ball against the fence,
The wall, the chopping block, the trees.
But never against the empty metal drums,
The wooden well, the sill, the double doors,
Never against the chancy echoing dark.

John Haislip

Incident in a Rose Garden

Gardener: Sir, I encountered Death
Just now among our roses.
Thin as a scythe he stood there.

I knew him by his pictures.
He had his black coat on,
Black gloves, a broad black hat.

I think he would have spoken,
Seeing his mouth stood open.
Big it was, with white teeth.

As soon as he beckoned, I ran.
I ran until I found you.
Sir, I am quitting my job.

I want to see my sons
Once more before I die.
I want to see California.

Master: Sir, you must be that stranger
Who threatened my gardener.
This is my property, sir.

I welcome only friends here.
Death: Sir, I knew your father.
And we were friends at the end.

As for your gardener,
I did not threaten him.
Old men mistake my gestures.

I only meant to ask him
To show me to his master.
I take it you are he?

Donald Justice

The Day We Die

The day we die
the wind comes down
to take away
our footprints.

The wind makes dust
to cover up
the marks we left
while walking.

For otherwise
the thing would seem
as if we were
still living.

Therefore the wind
is he who comes
to blow away
our footprints.

Kalahari origin (Africa)

Translated by Arthur Markowitz

Today Is a Very Good Day to Die

Today is a very good day to die.
Every living thing is in harmony with me.
Every voice sings a chorus within me.
All beauty has come to rest in my eyes.
All bad thoughts have departed from me.
Today is a very good day to die.
My land is peaceful around me.
My fields have been turned for the last time.
My house is filled with laughter.
My children have come home.
Yes, today is a very good day to die.

Nancy Wood

HEAVEN AND HELL

And when we die at last,
we really know very little about what happens then.
But people who dream
have often seen the dead appear to them
just as they were in life.
Therefore we believe life does not end here on earth.

We have heard of three places where men go after death:
There is the Land of the Sky, a good place
where there is no sorrow and fear.
There have been angatoks who went there
and came back to tell us about it:
They saw people playing ball, happy people
who did nothing but laugh and amuse themselves.
What we see from down here in the form of stars
are the lighted windows of the villages of the dead
in the Land of the Sky.

Then there are two other worlds of the dead underground:
Way deep down is a place just like here on earth
except on earth you starve
and down there they live in plenty.
The caribou graze in great herds
and there are endless plains
with juicy berries that are nice to eat.
Down there too, everything
is happiness and fun for the dead.

But there is another place, the Land of the Miserable,
right under the surface of the earth we walk on.
There go all the lazy men who were poor hunters,
and all women who refused to be tattooed,
not caring to suffer a little to become beautiful.
They had no life in them when they lived
so now after death they must squat on their haunches
with hanging heads, bad-tempered and silent,
and live in hunger and idleness
because they wasted their lives.
Only when a butterfly comes flying by
do they lift their heads
(as young birds open pink mouths uselessly after a gnat)
and when they snap at it, a puff of dust
comes out of their dry throats.

Of course it may be
that all I have been telling you is wrong
for you cannot be certain about what you cannot see.
But these are the stories that our people tell.

Netsilik origin (Eskimo)   Translated by Edward Field

The Artist

Mr. T
         bareheaded
                in a soiled undershirt
his hair standing out
         on all sides
                stood on his toes
heels together
         arms gracefully
                for the moment
curled above his head!
         Then he whirled about
                bounded
into the air
         and with an entrechat
                perfectly achieved
completed the figure.
         My mother
                taken by surprise
where she sat
         in her invalid's chair
                was left speechless.
"Bravo!" she cried at last
         and clapped her hands.
                The man's wife
came from the kitchen:
         "What goes on here?" she said.
                But the show was over.

William Carlos Williams

jumped
off

jumped off
the garage once
& landed both
ways
on my feet
like a cat
& on my head
like any dumb animal

thought i was
superman or
rocketman maybe
& i guess
everybody wants
to fly sometime
even if your
wings take you
straight down

Don Gray

Plea

To my friend
who can no longer see
animals in the clouds

and takes it
as a sign of madness:

Hang on. Keep watch.

They must be gathering now
over the Pacific,

great, soft herds of elephants,
cirrous alligators
and horses being pulled apart

with no pain.

Judith Hemschemeyer

Piano Lessons

i used to sit at piano lessons
and cry
or hear my sisters crying
in the other room.
the old woman would snap
and say tight-lipped
"you are no good. what is wrong
with you."
but every year she would invite us
to her dogs' birthday party.
only the dogs got hats.
and in the summer
her funny smell would fill
the screen porch
where we waited our turns
to be defeated.
i would sit in the hammock
with the green terry cover,
and the candy in those
crystal dishes
(we never really knew if it
was there to eat)
it always tasted a million years old.

Candy Clayton

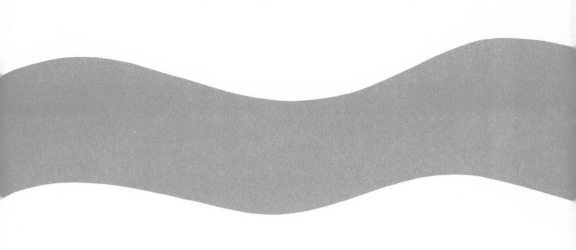

RIDING LESSON

I learned two things
from an early riding teacher.
He held a nervous filly
in one hand and gestured
with the other, saying, "Listen.
Keep one leg on one side,
the other leg on the other side,
and your mind in the middle."

He turned and mounted.
She took two steps, then left
the ground, I thought for good.
But she came down hard, humped
her back, swallowed her neck,
and threw her rider as you'd
throw a rock. He rose, brushed
his pants and caught his breath,
and said, "See, that's the way
to do it. When you see
they're gonna throw you, get off."

Henry Taylor

How to Paint
the Portrait of a Bird

First paint a cage
with an open door
then paint
something pretty
something simple
something fine
something useful
for the bird
next place the canvas against a tree
in a garden
in a wood
or in a forest
hide behind the tree
without speaking
without moving . . .
Sometimes the bird comes quickly
but it can also take many years
before making up its mind
Don't be discouraged
wait
wait if necessary for years
the quickness or the slowness of the coming
of the bird having no relation
to the success of the picture

When the bird comes
if it comes
observe the deepest silence
wait for the bird to enter the cage
and when it has entered
gently close the door with the paint-brush
then
one by one paint out all the bars
taking care not to touch one feather of the bird
Next make a portrait of the tree
choosing the finest of its branches
for the bird
paint also the green leaves and the freshness of the wind
dust in the sun
and the sound of the insects in the summer grass
and wait for the bird to decide to sing
If the bird does not sing
it is a bad sign
a sign that the picture is bad
but if it sings it is a good sign
a sign that you are ready to sign
so then you pluck very gently
one of the quills of the bird
and you write your name in a corner of the picture.

Jacques Prévert   Translated by Paul Dehn

400-METER FREESTYLE

THE GUN full swing the swimmer catapults and cracks

                    s

                     i

                    x

feet away onto that perfect glass he catches at

a

n

d

throws behind him scoop after scoop cunningly moving

                    t

                    h

                    e

water back to move him forward. Thrift is his wonderful

s

e

c

ret; he has schooled out all extravagance. No muscle

                    r

                    i

                    p

ples without compensation wrist cock to heel snap to

h

i

s

mobile mouth that siphons in the air that nurtures

                    h

                    i

                    m

at half an inch above sea level so to speak.

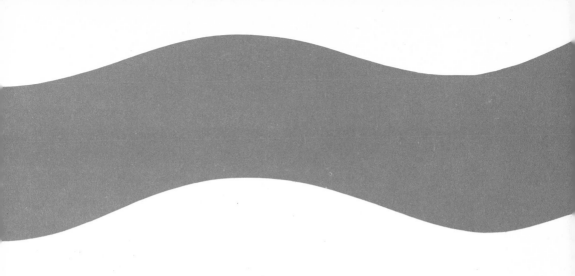

T
h
e
astonishing   whites   of   the   soles   of   his   feet   rise
a
n
d
salute   us   on   the   turns.   He   flips,   converts,   and   is   gone
a
l
l
in   one.   We   watch   him   for   signs.   His   arms   are   steady   at
t
h
e
catch,   his   cadent   feet   tick   in   the   stretch,   they   know
t
h
e
lesson   well. Lungs   know,   too;   he   does   not   list   for
a
i
r
he   drives   along   on   little   sips   carefully   expended
b
u
t
that   plum   red   heart   pumps   hard   cries   hurt   how   soon
i
t
s
near one more and makes its final surge   TIME: 4:25:9

Maxine Kumin   57

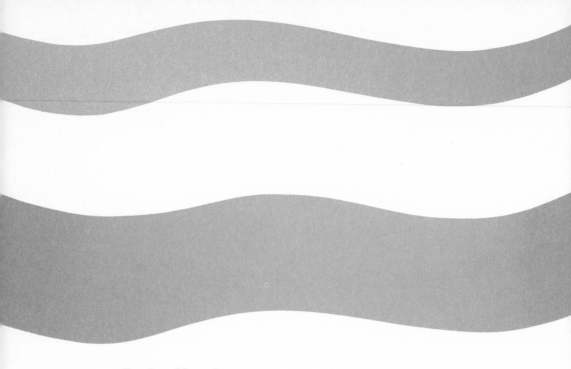

Pole Vault

He is running like a wasp,
Hanging on a long pole.
As a matter of course he floats in the sky,
Chasing the ascending horizon.
Now he has crossed the limit,
And pushed away his support.
For him there is nothing but a descent.
Oh, he falls helplessly.
Now on that runner, awkwardly fallen on the ground,
Once more
The horizon comes down,
Beating hard on his shoulders.

Shiro Murano

Translated by Satoru Sato
and Constance Urdang

Sky Diving

In the engine sound like many people together
beating and singing at incredible speed
to find a way out of the body into flight
and the spirit, I sit
strapped up and buckled, feeling my blood
beat hard in my fingers, temples
and lips. I have climbed my fear
to this place
to die a little and be born
a little in the air.

Twelve thousand feet, thinking more
now of my weight
than ever before, and it is hard to lift
my arms, though in a moment
I must. The others tell me
not to look out the window, so I do not move
from the corner
where the fuselage against my back easily becomes
a wall, and we are all sitting
in a small whistling room
not talking much
to each other.

Two and a half miles is a long
fall, but I have fallen
farther
with nearly as much
to lose.
I am almost ready. I am ready. I will
stand and walk out the door, surprised
to see what is really there and go
down without breathing, with a strange
good sensation
in my groin.

Rod Taylor

What My Uncle Tony Told My Sister, Angie, and Me

respect your mother and father
respect your brothers and sisters
respect your uncles and aunts
respect your land, the beginning
respect what is taught you
respect what you are named
respect the gods
respect yourself
everything that is around you
is part of you.

Simon J. Ortiz

SELF EXPRESSION

Mother has caught her head
in the bubble-gum machine
looking for her purple leotard.
Her black one she's saving
for funerals, she said.
Now if someone will answer her ad
and return her feather boa
constrictor, maybe she will stop
sharpening her fingers
and begin to cook again.

Ann Darr

You Had to Go to Funerals

You had to go to funerals
Even if you didn't know the
People
Your Mama always did
Usually your Pa.
In new patent leather shoes
It wasn't so bad
And if it rained
The graves dropped open
And if the sun was shining
You could take some of the
Flowers home
In your pocket
Book. At six and seven
The face in a gray box
Is always your daddy's
Old schoolmate
Mowed down before his
Time.
You don't even ask
After a while
What makes them lie so
Awfully straight
And still. If there's a picture of
Jesus underneath
The coffin lid
You might, during a boring sermon,
Without shouting or anything
Wonder who painted it

And how he would like
All eternity to stare
It down.   *Alice Walker*

Have You Ever Hurt About Baskets?

Have you ever hurt about
baskets?

I have, seeing my grandmother
weaving for a long time.

Have you ever hurt about work?
I have because my father works
too hard and he tells how
he works.

Have you ever hurt about cattle?
I have because my grandfather
has been working on the cattle
for a long time.

Have you ever hurt about school?

I have because I have learned
lots of words from school,
and they are not my words.

Marylita Altaha

Lineage

My grandmothers were strong.
They followed plows and bent to toil.
They moved through fields sowing seed.
They touched earth and grain grew.
They were full of sturdiness and singing.
My grandmothers were strong.

My grandmothers are full of memories
Smelling of soap and onions and wet clay
With veins rolling roughly over quick hands
They have many clean words to say.
My grandmothers were strong.
Why am I not as they?

Margaret Walker

THE CHINESE GREENGROCERS

They live their days in a fragrance
of white and black grapes
and tomatoes and the fresh
water smell of lettuce.

They know with their hands
and noses the value
of all things grown.
They will make you a bargain price
on overripe cantaloupe.

They wash with clear water
their bunches of carrots
and radishes. They crank out
a canvas awning to shelter them.

Their babies suckle on unsold bananas.
By the age of six
they can all make change
and tell which fruits are ripe.

The grandmothers know only numbers
in English, and the names
of fruits and vegetables.

They open before the supermarkets open,
they are open all day,
they eat with an eye on the door.

They keep sharp eyes
for shoplifting children.
They know every customer's
brand of cigarettes.

After the neighbourhood movies are out
and the drugstores have all closed
they bring in their blueberries
and cabbages and potted flowers.

In the rooms behind the store
they speak in their own language.
Their speech flies around the rooms
like swooping, pecking birds.

Far into the night I believe
they weigh balsa baskets
of plums, count ears of corn
and green peppers.

No matter how they may wash
their fingers, their very pores
are perfumed with green,
and they sleep with parsley and peaches
oranges and onions
and grapes and running water.

Pat Lowther

Game After Supper

This is before electricity,
it is when there were porches.

On the sagging porch an old man
is rocking. The porch is wooden,

the house is wooden and grey;
in the living room which smells of
smoke and mildew, soon
the woman will light the kerosene lamp.

There is a barn but I am not in the barn;
there is an orchard too, gone bad,
its apples like soft cork
but I am not there either.

I am hiding in the long grass
with my two dead cousins,
the membrane grown already
across their throats.

We hear crickets and our own hearts
close to our ears;
though we giggle, we are afraid.

From the shadows around
the corner of the house
a tall man is coming to find us:

He will be an uncle,
if we are lucky.

Margaret Atwood

PROSPECTUS

I was raised on the Reservation
In an adobe house, with neither
A running water.
My bed was cradleboard
A sheepskin and the earth.
My food was my Mother's breast,
Goat's milk and cornmeal.
My play partners were puppies,
The lamb and the lizards.
I ate with my fingers,
I went barefoot at most time,
I washed my hair with yucca roots,
I carried water from the ditch.
My Mom ground corn for food.
Sometimes I went without eating.
I only spoke my language.
I prayed to the Great Spirit.
Someday I'll learn to speak English.

Joe Nieto

Kit, Six Years Old,
Standing by the Dashboard
Keeping Daddy Awake
on a Trip Home from the Beach

We'd have a old car, the kind that gets
flat tires, but inside would be wolfskin on
the seats and warm fur on the steering wheel,
and wolf fur on all the buttons. And we'd
live in a ranch house made out of logs with
a loft where you sleep, and you'd walk a
little ways and there'd be the farm with
the horses. We'd drive to town, and we'd
have flat tires, and be sort of old.

William Stafford

ANCESTORS

On the wind-beaten plains
once lived my ancestors.

In the days of peaceful moods,
they wandered and hunted.

In days of need or greed,
they warred and loafed.

Beneath the lazy sun, kind winds above,
they laughed and feasted.

Through the starlit night, under the moon,
they dreamed and loved.

Now, from the wind-beaten plains,
only their dust rises.

Grey Cohoe

The Giveaway

Saint Bridget was
A problem child.
Although a lass
Demure and mild,
And one who strove
To please her dad,
Saint Bridget drove
The family mad.
For here's the fault in Bridget lay:
She would *give everything away*.

To any soul
Whose luck was out
She'd give her bowl
Of stirabout;
She'd give her shawl,
Divide her purse
With one or all.
And what was worse,
When she ran out of things to give
She'd borrow from a relative.

Her father's gold,
Her grandsire's dinner,
She'd hand to cold
And hungry sinner;
Give wine, give meat,
No matter whose;
Take from her feet
The very shoes,
And when her shoes had gone to others,
Fetch forth her sister's and her mother's.

She could not quit.
She had to share;
Gave bit by bit
The silverware,
The barnyard geese,
The parlor rug,
Her little niece-
'S christening mug,
Even her bed to those in want,
And then the mattress of her aunt.

An easy touch
For poor and lowly,
She gave so much
And grew so holy
That when she died
Of years and fame,
The countryside
Put on her name,
And still the Isles of Erin fidget
With generous girls named Bride or Bridget.

Well, one must love her.
Nonetheless,
In thinking of her
Givingness,
There's no denial
She must have been
A sort of trial
To her kin.
The moral, too, seems rather quaint.
Who had the patience of a saint,
From evidence presented here?
Saint Bridget? Or her near and dear?

Phyllis McGinley

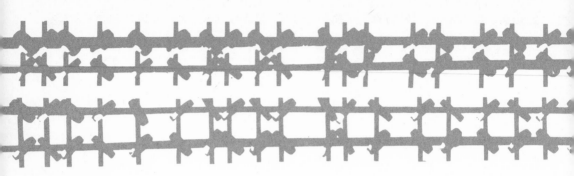

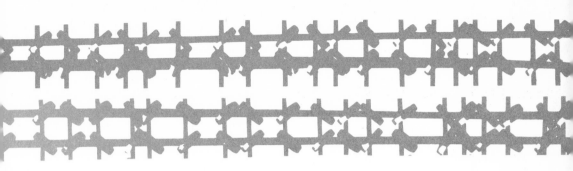

Love Song for a Jellyfish

How amazed I was, when I was a child,
To see your life on the sand.
To see you living in your jelly shape,
Round and slippery and dangerous.
You seemed to have fallen
Not from the rim of the sea,
But from the galaxies.
Stranger, you delighted me. Weird object of
The stinging world.

Sandra Hochman

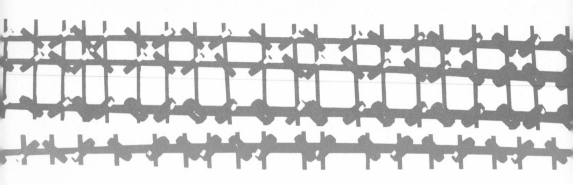

Flying Crooked

The butterfly, a cabbage-white,
(His honest idiocy of flight)
Will never now, it is too late,
Master the art of flying straight,
Yet has—who knows so well as I?—
A just sense of how not to fly:
He lurches here and here by guess
And God and hope and hopelessness.
Even the aerobatic swift
Has not his flying-crooked gift.

Robert Graves

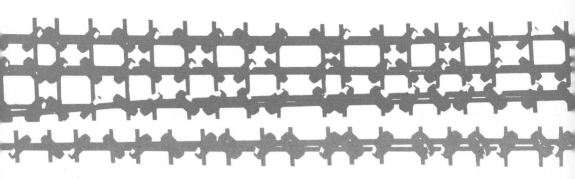

Pigeons

They paddle with staccato feet
in powder-pools of sunlight,
small blue busybodies
strutting like fat gentlemen
with hands clasped
under their swallowtail coats;
and as they stump about,
their heads like tiny hammers
tap at imaginary nails
in non-existent walls.

Elusive ghosts of sunshine
slither down the green gloss
of their necks an instant, and are gone.

Summer hangs drugged from sky to earth
in limpid fathoms of silence:
only warm dark dimples of sound
slide like slow bubbles
from the contented throats.

Raise a casual hand—
with one quick gust
they fountain into air.

Richard Kell

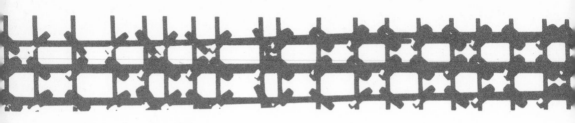

The
Cat

While you read
the sleepmoth begins
to circle your eyes
and then—
a hail of claws
lands the cat
in your lap.
The little motor
in his throat
is how a cat says
Me. He rasps the soft
file of his tongue
along the inside
of your wrist.
He licks himself.
He's building
a pebble of fur
in his stomach.
And now he pulls
his body in a circle
around the fire of sleep.

William Matthews

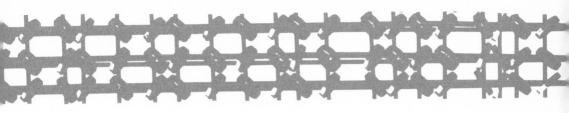

FELINE LESSON

We watched slant-eyes
come over the fence
and drop with a thump
on the barbered lawn.
Crouched under the gardenia,
he began the interrogation of
a prize-some tiny field
mouse hardly worth the
effort, it would seem,
to tease and pat and fawn
to excite his lust.

When we approached,
he took it almost all,
leaving just the sliver of
a tail outside his mouth.
He would not obey, of course,
and hunched and held,
wary-eyed against persuasion.

The mouse was not our pet,
and I knew well the cat.
What else could you expect of him?
But still my youngest son
cried half the night away.

Hugh McNamar

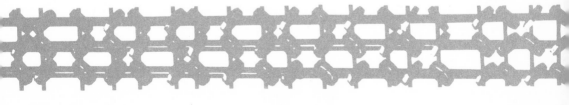

THE SHARK

My dear, let me tell you about the shark.
Though his eyes are bright, his thought is dark.
He's quiet—that speaks well of him.
So does the fact that he can swim.
But though he swims without a sound,
Wherever he swims he looks around
With those two bright eyes and that one dark thought.
He has only one but he thinks it a lot.
And the thought he thinks but can never complete
Is his long dark thought of something to eat.
Most anything does. And I have to add
That when he eats his manners are bad.
He's a gulper, a ripper, a snatcher, a grabber.
Yes, his manners are drab. But his thought is drabber.
That one dark thought he can never complete
Of something—anything—somehow to eat.

Be careful where you swim, my sweet.

John Ciardi

SARDINES

A baby Sardine
Saw her first submarine:
She was scared and watched through a peephole.

"Oh, come, come, come,"
Said the Sardine's mum,
"It's only a tin full of people."

Spike Milligan

The Duck

Behold the duck.
It does not cluck.
A cluck it lacks.
It quacks.
It is specially fond
Of a puddle or pond.
When it dines or sups,
It bottoms ups.

Ogden Nash

The little bat hangs upside down,
And downside up the possum.
To show a smile they have to frown,
Say those who've run across'em.

David McCord

While
the Snake Sleeps

his dinner sits
in his stomach
bathing in acid

snake's tail is flat
his head is flat
his ribs in front and back
of his dinner are flat

his lidless eyes
turn in on themselves
his tongue rests
in his mouth

Judith Sampson

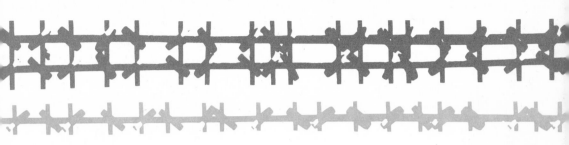

Snake Hunt

David Wagoner

On sloping, shattered granite, the snake man
From the zoo bent over the half-shaded crannies
Where rattlesnakes take turns out of the sun,
Stared hard, nodded at me, then lunged
With his thick gloves and yanked one up like a root.

And the whole hillside sprang to death with a hissing,
Metallic, chattering rattle; they came out writhing
In his fists, uncoiling from daydreams,
Pale bellies looping out of darker diamonds
In the shredded sunlight, dropping into his sack.

As I knelt on rocks, my blood went cold as theirs.
One snake coughed up a mouse. I saw what a mouse
Knows, as well as anyone. There, beside me,
In a cleft a foot away from my braced fingers,
Still in its coils, a rattler stirred from sleep.

It moved the wedge of its head back into shadow
And stared at me, harder than I could answer,
Till the gloves came down between us. In the sack,
Like the disembodied muscles of a torso,
It and the others searched among themselves

For the lost good place. I saw them later
Behind plate glass, wearing their last skins.
They held their venom behind wide-open eyes.

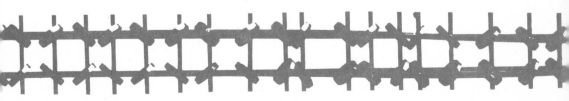

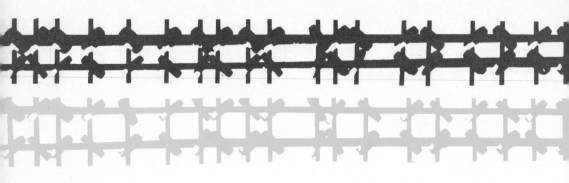

ZOO

Evolution dies out.
The cats fall as they are born
To sleep, without movement
To go after, movement to catch
Their deadly fascination.
Without wild heat
Rippling the distance, stripes
Rest easy on the zebra.
Gazelle are safe with nowhere
To run. There is only a flicker
Of something in the shudder of muscle
Fighting off the flies.

Michael Allin

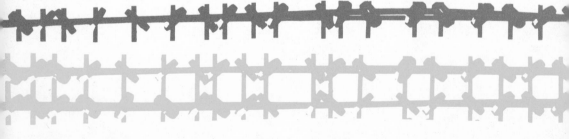

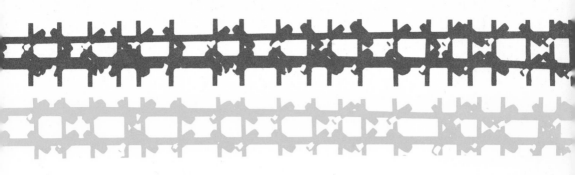

THE FALL

The European Bison fell from grace.
So did the white-tailed Gnu.
Likewise the Blesbok, as also the Mountain Zebra.
The Giant Tortoise must have sinned too.

Everyone knows about the Dodo;
The same goes for the Great Auk.
The inoffensive Okapi's crime
Was trying to be other beasts at the same time.
And there is the case of the Blue-Buck.

They all came to a halt and are dissolved in mystery.
Who remembers, now, Steller's cullionly Sea-Cow?
It, too, through its innocent fault
Failed the finals in history.

Muriel Spark

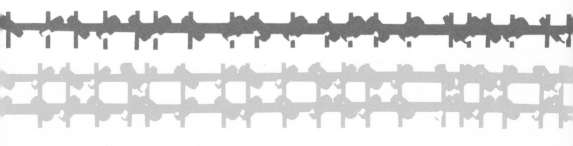

THROUGH THE WINDOW

Through the window
I see the soft rain.

Through the soft rain
I see the neighbor's fence.

And just above the fence
I see fully opened umbrellas
Softly flowing from left to right
On and on.

Hidden by the neighbor's fence
I can not see
Who goes there
Under each of the umbrellas.

But, I see each umbrella
Softly flowing from left to right
On and on,
Shading the someone under it
In the soft morning rain.

Naoshi Koriyama

The Driver

Someday I'm going to pick up
An east-bound hitchhiker and take him
Wherever he wants to go.
I'll ask him where he's headed
And he'll say "Boston"
And I'll say "Boston it is."

He'll probably think twice
About riding with me, then.
But after a while
He'll see that I'm normal
And we'll get to Boston
And I'll say "so long"
And he'll no longer exist
For me.

I'll pick up two girls
Who are headed for California,
And say "California it is."
They'll think twice because
They'll know that I'm normal.
But after a while they'll
See that I only intend to
Take them wherever they want to go
And I'll leave them in L.A.
Or San Francisco and say
"So long" and they'll cease
To exist for me.

So I'll spend my whole life
Giving rides to people
Who couldn't exist where
They found themselves living.
I'll go all directions
And never take money.
And I'll die when I
Pick up the killer.

Joel Lueders

Isleta Indian Girl

smooth dark eyes, wanting
touches me, looking at her,
so small, each gesture a
reaching

little animals move
through forests the way
she folds her paper, sighs,
lips murmuring apologies
for her poor English she
follows surely out of
this room a trail older
than any university: most
languages would take note
of those simple graces.

Keith Wilson

After Supper

After supper I would trail
the scrape and thump of my brothers'
boots across the yard
to where it met the pasture;
both were really one
except one nearer,
the other more important.

Watching the cattle feed, my brothers
could talk an hour. Men governed by the seasons,
they could speak of hay to gather
before the rain—
but not too soon, a well marked Holstein,
those still with calves to suck.
As meadowlarks called from
somewhere along the fence-row,
the favorites were
watched with reverence as they fed.
There was communion while those
closest to the fence
allowed their foreheads to be stroked.

To me, though, listening
on those evenings,
they still stood just spotted brutes,
flinching beneath their flies.

Hugh McNamar

Looking North to Taos

I saw the pueblo beneath the blue
mountain, the older
buildings crumbling,
melting into mud. I watched
the old men, their heads
hidden beneath blankets,
and I wondered.

I have heard the round dance songs
from a thousand miles away,
have held the record cover in my
hands and seen the young boys
pictured on the back, their braids
long, their smiles not showing.
And I have wondered.

I sit still in the cool grass
toward evening,
legs crossed and tongue silent,
thinking as I look into the
dancing supper fires, "Am I
an Indian?" And I wonder.

Rudy Bantista

Religion

I'm a believer.
  I believe in kids
  Who ride their bikes
  Without holding on.

  I believe in the chances
  We take.
  To be complete
  For one moment
  With something we need.

  I believe in the crawling
  And struggling
  Of a baby
  Much more than I believe
  In his first step.

  I believe in trees,
  Especially willows,
  That do not try to fight the wind.

  And I believe in you,
  Whoever you are.
I believe.

Merrit Malloy

Breaklight

light keeps on breaking
i keep knowing
the language of other nations.
i keep hearing
tree talk
water words
and i keep knowing what they mean.
and light just keeps on breaking.
last night
the fears of my mother came
knocking and when i
opened the door
they tried to explain themselves
and i understood
everything they said.

Lucille Clifton

Weather

On sunny afternoons
baby carriages gather
outside launderettes
to plot their escape.

On cold mornings
large men at bus stops
stand like old smudge pots
waiting to be collected.

On hot nights
windows open
like sleepy eyes
and people hear
each other's music.

Robert Hershon

How to Tell a Tornado

Listen for noises.
If you do not live
near railroad tracks,
the freight train you hear
is not the Northern Pacific
lost in the storm:
that is a tornado
doing imitations of itself.
One of its favorite sounds
is no sound.
After the high wind, and
before the freight train,
there is a pocket of nothing:
this is when you think
everything has stopped:
do not be fooled.
Leave it all behind
except for a candle
and take to the cellar

Afterwards
if straws are imbedded
in trees without leave,
and your house—except
for the unbroken bathroom mirror—
has vanished
without a trace,
and you are naked
except for the right leg
of your pants,
you can safely assume
that a tornado
has gone through your life
without touching it.

Howard Mohr

Nothing at All

A cellar and an attic are friends
the cellar works hard for his keep
and has for his pains a furnace in his throat
and a bellyful of boiling water
the attic sits in the clouds from morning to night
with nothing at all in his head
but a rocking horse and a broken chair

from time to time the attic speaks of going away
sick of the bickering maples
sick of distance
sick of the gaping sky
he would get a place in the city
How can you bear me *he sighs*

the cellar shrugs No no
it's nothing at all
he wallows in the earth
like an ark of stone in a windless sea
nor will he take the attic seriously

one night a storm comes bellowing down from the hills
looking for trouble
its mane crackles with flame
rain drools from its jowls
it takes the house in its teeth and shakes it
from side
to side

a while the friends hold fast
but the attic
weak from want of exercise
lets go in the end
rising like a bat on great ungainly wings
he clatters away over the horrified maples

in time the storm grows bored and mutters off
the cellar crouches in the cooling mire
the fire in his throat is out
his belly gives him peace at last
but through the cracks he watches the sky
for the first time open
its clear blue idiot eye
and sees to the back of heaven
nothing at all
not a sheltering cloud
not a shadow
not a broken chair
the maples drop a few last tears and doze in the sun

Donald Finkel

Hello, Hello Henry

My neighbor in the country, Henry Manley,
with a washpot warming on his woodstove,
with a heifer and two goats and yearly chickens,
has outlasted Stalin, Roosevelt and Churchill
but something's stirring in him in his dotage.

Last fall he dug a hole and moved his privy
and a year ago in April reamed his well out.
When the county sent a truck and poles and cable,
his *Daddy* ran the linemen off with birdshot
and swore he'd die by oil lamp, and did.

Now you tell me that all yesterday in Boston
you set your city phone at mine, and had it ringing
inside a dead apartment for three hours
room after empty room, to keep yours busy.
I hear it in my head, that ranting summons.

That must have been about the time that Henry
walked up two miles, shy as a girl come calling
to tell me he has a phone now, 264, ring two.
It rang one time last week—wrong number.
He'd be pleased if one day I would think to call him.

Hello, hello Henry? Is that you?

Maxine Kumin

Poem

I loved my friend.
He went away from me.
There's nothing more to say.
The poem ends,
Soft as it began—
I loved my friend.

Langston Hughes

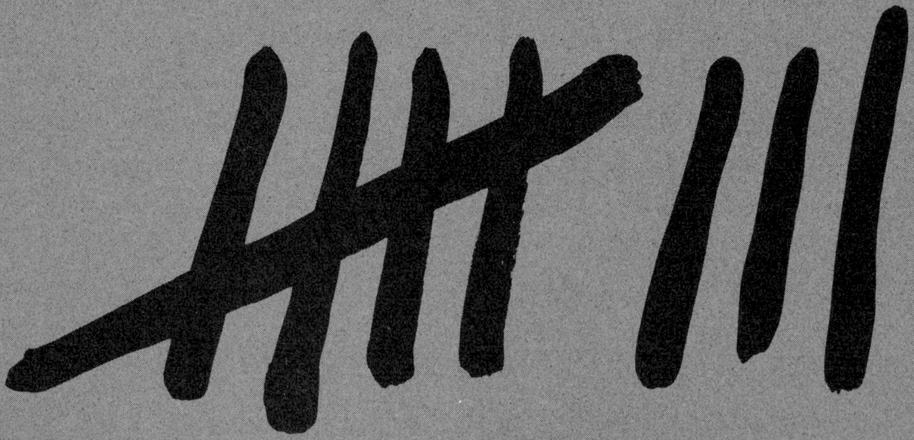

Worms and the Wind

Worms would rather be worms.
Ask a worm and he says, "Who knows what a worm knows?"
Worms go down and up and over and under.
Worms like tunnels.
When worms talk they talk about the worm world.
Worms like it in the dark.
Neither the sun nor the moon interests a worm.
Zigzag worms hate circle worms.
Curve worms never trust square worms.
Worms know what worms want.
Slide worms are suspicious of crawl worms.
One worm asks another, "How does your belly drag today?"
The shape of a crooked worm satisfies a crooked worm.
A straight worm says, "Why not be straight?"
Worms tired of crawling begin to slither.
Long worms slither farther than short worms.
Middle-sized worms say, "It is nice to be neither long nor short."
Old worms teach young worms to say, "Don't be sorry for me unless you
    have been a worm and lived in worm places and read worm books."
When worms go to war they dig in, come out and fight, dig in again,
    come out and fight again, dig in again, and so on.
Worms underground never hear the wind overground and sometimes they
    ask, "What is this wind we hear of?"

Carl Sandburg

Race Prejudice

Little mouse:
Are you
some rat's little child?
I won't love you if you are.

Alfred Kreymborg

MIGRATION

She stood hanging wash before sun
and occasionally watched the kids
gather acorns from the trees,
and when her husband came,
complaining about the tobacco spit on him
they decided to run North
for a free evening.
She stood hanging wash in the basement
and saw the kids sneak puffs from cigarettes,
fix steel traps with cheese
and when her husband came,
complaining of the mill's drudgery,
         she burst—
said he had no hunter's heart
beat him with a broom,
became blinded by the orange sun
racing into steel mill flames
and afterwards,
sat singing spirituals to sons.

Carole Gregory Clemmons

Done With

My house is torn down—
Plaster sifting, the pillars broken,
Beams jagged, the wall crushed by the bulldozer.
The whole roof has fallen
On the hall and the kitchen
The bedrooms, the parlor.

They are trampling the garden—
My mother's lilac, my father's grapevine,
The freesias, the jonquils, the grasses.
Hot asphalt goes down
Over the torn stems, and hardens.

What will they do in springtime
Those bulbs and stems groping upward
That drown in earth under the paving,
Thick with sap, pale in the dark
As they try the unrolling of green.

May they double themselves
Pushing together up to the sunlight,
May they break through the seal stretched above them
Open and flower and cry we are living.

Ann Stanford

Roaches

Last night when I got up
to let the dog out I spied
a cockroach in the bathroom
crouched flat on the cool
            porcelain,
                    delicate
antennae probing the toothpaste cap
        and feasting himself on a gob
            of it in the bowl:
I killed him with one unprofessional
                    blow,
scattering arms and legs
        and half his body in the sink . . .

I would have no truck with roaches,
crouched like lions in the ledges of sewers
their black eyes in the darkness
                    alert for tasty slime,
breeding quickly and without design,
laboring up drainpipes through filth
                        to the light;
I read once they are among
        the most antediluvian of creatures,
        surviving everything,
        and in more primitive times
thrived to the size of your hand . . .

yet when sinking asleep
        or craning at the stars,
I can feel their light feet
                probing in my veins,
their whiskers nibbling
                the insides of my toes;
and neck arched,
        feel their patient scrambling
up the dark tubes of my throat.   Peter Wild

Battle Won Is Lost

They said, "You are no longer a lad."
    I nodded.
They said, "Enter the council lodge."
    I sat.
They said, "Our lands are at stake."
    I scowled.
They said, "We are at war."
    I hated.
They said, "Prepare red war symbols."
    I painted.
They said, "Count coups."
    I scalped.
They said, "You'll see friends die."
    I cringed.
They said, "Desperate warriors fight best."
    I charged.
They said, "Some will be wounded."
    I bled.
They said, "To die is glorious."
    They lied.

Phil George

The Locust Swarm

Locusts laid their eggs in the corpse
Of a soldier. When the worms were
Mature, they took wing. Their drone
Was ominous, their shells hard.
Anyone could tell they had hatched
From an unsatisfied anger.
They flew swiftly towards the North.
They hid the sky like a curtain.
When the wife of the soldier
Saw them, she turned pale, her breath
Failed her. She knew he was dead
In battle, his corpse lost in
The desert. That night she dreamed
She rode a white horse, so swift
It left no footprints, and came
To where he lay in the sand.
She looked at his face, eaten
By the locusts, and tears of
Blood filled her eyes. Ever after
She would not let her children
Injure any insect which
Might have fed on the dead. She
Would lift her face to the sky
And say, "O locusts, if you
Are seeking a place to winter,
You can find shelter in my heart."

Hsu Chao

The Wolves

Last night knives flashed. LeChien cried
And chewed blood in his bed.
Vanni's whittling blade
Had found flesh easier than wood.

Vanni and I left camp on foot. In a glade
We came on a brown blossom
Great and shining on a thorned stem.
"That's the sensitive brier," I said.

"It shrinks at the touch," I added.
Soon we found buffalo. Picking
A bull grazing by itself, I began
The approach: while the shaggy head

Was turned I sprinted across the sod,
And when he swung around his gaze
I bellyflopped in the grass
And lay on my heartbeat and waited.

When he looked away again I made
Enough yardage before he wheeled
His head: I kneeled, leveled
My rifle, and we calmly waited.

It occurred to me as we waited
That in those last moments he was,
In fact, daydreaming about something else.
"He is too stupid to live," I said.

His legs shifted and the heart showed.
I fired. He looked, trotted off,
He simply looked and trotted off,
Stumbled, sat himself down, and became dead.

I looked for Vanni. Amid the cows he stood,
Only his arms moving as he fired,
Loaded, and fired, the dumb herd
Milling about him sniffing at their dead.

I called and he retreated.
We cut two choice tongues for ourselves
And left the surplus. All day wolves
Would splash blood from those great sides.

Again we saw the flower, brown-red
On a thorn-spiked stem. When Vanni
Extended his fingers, it was funny,
It shrank away as if it had just died.

They told us in camp that LeChien was dead.
None of us cared. Nobody much
Had liked him. His tobacco pouch,
I observed, was already missing from beside his bed.

Galway Kinnell

Plaint of the Summer Vampires

DEERFLY   Winged sizzling pellet am I
and mottled flat triangle. Shrieking
blood-lust animates me as Soul
Body her pupa. My meal is the thin pain
where your hair divides in oil, my life a headlong
hurtling upon crowns of heads—your own
succulent head, the huge hard
unswishable heads of horses. You are wrong
to hate me; if I torment you
that is my doom.

MOSQUITO   I am all thin: subtlety on a thin
whine, six cocked legs hair-fine;
your skin where they touch down
is thicker. I am all
pin-striped, pin-slender, head
a perfect pinhead, mouth whose tiny puncture
can slip between nerveends more needle-
sharp than any pin. Sweat
is my Siren scent, my greed is boundless
witless and impersonal, my nature
none of my choosing.

TOGETHER   O to turn aphid! O
for unresistant leaf-juices and no
murderous mammoth hands whacking! Never to be
tangled again in hair or spotted on your wrist
sipping, and no chance for a getaway.
—Though you knock ME senseless a dozen times—
—Or flail *me* away—what can we do
but sort our wings and legs and try again
again and yet again? Starve or be slapped to death
is what it comes to. Pity us.
The thirst for blood is a curse.   Judith Moffett

Waking

I said to myself one morning:
   "Annie, the world is fair;
You'd better be up and combing
   The tangles out of your hair."

Quickly myself made answer:
   "The world is horrid and queer,
And if you don't go to sleep again
   You're going to be sorry, dear."

Annie Higgins

Alarm Clock

in the deep sleep forest
there were ferns
there were feathers
there was fur
and a soft ripe peach
on a branch within my

       r-r-r-r-r-r-r-r-r-r-r-r-r-r-r-r-r-r-r-r-r-r-r-r-r-r-r

Eve Merriam

FORMULA

To dream,
you don't have to ask permission,
nor cry out,
nor humble yourself,
nor put on lipstick;
it's enough to close your eyes halfway
and feel distant.
Perhaps the night dreams
that it is no longer night;
the fish, that they are boats;
the boats, fish;
the water, crystal.
To dream
is a simple thing;
it doesn't cost a cent,
you need only to turn your back
on the hours that pass
and cover over pain,
your ears,
your eyes
and stay so,
stay
until we are awakened
by a blow upon the soul.

Ana María Iza

Translated by Ron Connally

Two Ways to Wake a Sleepwalker

I

Not too abruptly, now;
any shock may start up
something none of us can
finish. Maybe a little
tug on his pajama sleeve
will serve. No sudden noises
please. I read somewhere
it's bad to bring them
out of it too suddenly.

He doesn't know what's
going on or where he's
headed. Give him some
direction or he'll simply
drift in mystery from
room to room. He doesn't
really see what lies
ahead of him. Best to
guide him back to bed.

When morning comes, he
won't remember anything.
We can joke about it
then. Best without a doubt
to keep him half asleep
and let him dream it out.

II

Kick him. Nothing like
a sudden jolt to bring him
out of that unearthly
lethargy. Can't stand
to see a human being
anything but wide awake—
much less this dumb body
going through such empty
mindless motions.

                                Slap
his stupid face until
he realizes who and
where he is. I bet he'll
thank us when he learns we
wouldn't stand for stupor.
Whole damn world is watching
every move we make, so
do it quick. There's
got to be some pain.

Kick him hard so he'll
remember who it was
that brought him howling
out of it and taught him
what it really means
to really be awake.

Edward Lueders

Preoccupation

Chaff is in my eye,
A crocodile has me by the leg,
A goat is in the garden,
A porcupine is cooking in the pot,
Meal is drying on the pounding rock,
The King has summoned me to court,
And I must go to the funeral of my mother-in-law:
In short, I am busy.

Mbundu origin (Africa)

Translated by Merlin Ennis

WHERE?

There's a place the man always say
Come in here, child
No cause you should weep
Wolf never catch the rabbit
Golden hair never turn white with grief
Come in here, child
No cause you should moan
Brother never hurt his brother
Nobody here ever wander without a home
There must be some such place somewhere
But I never heard of it.

Kenneth Patchen

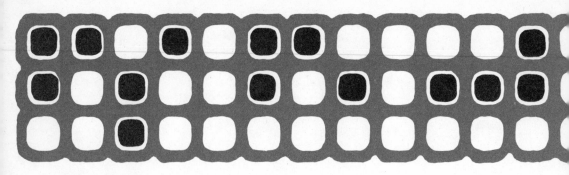

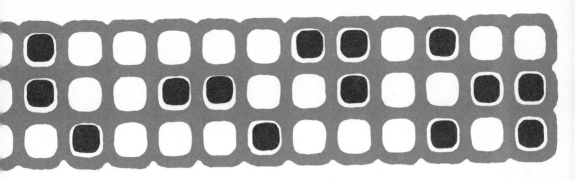

Explanations of Love

There is a place where love begins and a place
where love ends.

There is a touch of two hands that foils all
dictionaries.

There is a look of eyes fierce as a big Bethlehem open hearth
furnace or a little green-fire acetylene torch.

There are single careless bywords portentous as a
big bend in the Mississippi River.

Hands, eyes, bywords—out of these love makes
battlegrounds and workshops.

There is a pair of shoes love wears and the coming
is a mystery.

There is a warning love sends and the cost of it
is never written till long afterward.

There are explanations of love in all languages
and not one found wiser than this:

There is a place where love begins and a place
where love ends—and love asks nothing.

Carl Sandburg

With the Door Open

Something I want to communicate to you,
I keep my door open between us.
I am unable to say it,
I am happy only
with the door open between us.

David Ignatow

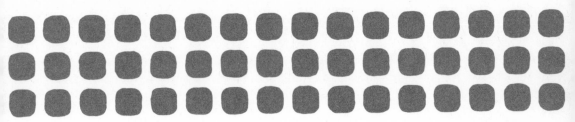

Simile

What did we say to each other
that now we are as the deer
who walk in single file
with heads high
with ears forward
with eyes watchful
with hooves always placed on firm ground
in whose limbs there is latent flight

N. Scott Momaday

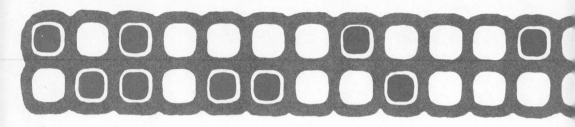

Water
Color

The painter puts two thin lines
On one side of the page,
And one line on the other side.
Suddenly grass grows there!

Between them, a wavering line.
Water is moving!

Your two eyes look at me.
You lift one hand.

Suddenly my heart is growing toward you.
Suddenly I am moving toward you!

Paul Engle

Simple-song

When we are going toward someone we say
you are just like me
your thoughts are my brothers
word matches word
how easy to be together.

When we are leaving someone we say
how strange you are
we cannot communicate
we can never agree
how hard, hard and weary to be together.

We are not different nor alike
but each strange in his leather body
sealed in skin and reaching out clumsy hands
and loving is an act
that cannot outlive
the open hand
the open eye
the door in the chest standing open.

Marge Piercy

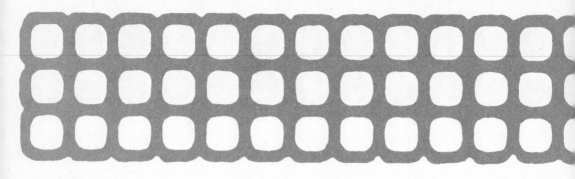

Mi Maestro

i wish
        you were
                    a sponge—
that i could
            wring
                    squeeze tightly
above my head;
With all
        the desire
                    that i have
to learn
        from you
                    about
                        me.

Ana Castillo

Separation

Your absence has gone through me
Like thread through a needle.
Everything I do is stitched with its color.

W. S. Merwin

Intimates

Don't you care for my love? she said bitterly.

I handed her the mirror, and said:
Please address these questions to the proper person!
Please make all requests to head-quarters!
In all matters of emotional importance
please approach the supreme authority direct!—
So I handed her the mirror.

And she would have broken it over my head,
but she caught sight of her own reflection
and that held her spellbound for two seconds
while I fled.

D. H. Lawrence

In Golden Gate Park That Day

In Golden Gate Park that day
      a man and his wife were coming along
  thru the enormous meadow
        which was the meadow of the world
He was wearing green suspenders
        and carrying an old beat-up flute
          in one hand
  while his wife had a bunch of grapes
        which she kept handing out
          individually
      to various squirrels
        as if each
        were a little joke

And then the two of them came on
        thru the enormous meadow
which was the meadow of the world
          and then
    at a very still spot where the trees dreamed
   and seemed to have been waiting thru all time
         for them
    they sat down together on the grass
       without looking at each other
   and ate oranges
       without looking at each other
        and put the peels
  in a basket which they seemed
     to have brought for that purpose
   without looking at each other

And then
      he took his shirt and undershirt off
   but kept his hat on
          sideways
           and without saying anything
    fell asleep under it
       And his wife just sat there looking
at the birds which flew about
   calling to each other
        in the stilly air
     as if they were questioning existence
     or trying to recall something forgotten

But then finally
    she too lay down flat
        and just lay there looking up
            at nothing
   yet fingering the old flute
         which nobody played
   and finally looking over
           at him
without any particular expression
       except a certain awful look
  of terrible depression

Lawrence Ferlinghetti

Haiku

*there are things sadder
than you and I. some people
do not even touch.*

Sonia Sanchez

My Rules

*If you want to marry me, here's what you'll have to do
You must learn how to make a perfect chicken dumpling stew
And you must sew my holey socks and you must soothe my troubled mind
And develop the knack for scratching my back
And keep my shoes spotlessly shined
And while I rest you must rake up the leaves
And when it is hailing and snowing
You must shovel the walk, and be still when I talk
And—hey, where are you going??*

Shel Silverstein

I Love You in Caves and Meadows

I love you in caves and meadows.
Flying, I love you.
In parks and streets and alleys I love you.
By the bones of my mother,
by the clenched fist of my father,
by sunlight and by starlight
by moonlight and by lamplight
by phosphorus match
and by fire lit of dated newspapers,
by fire of dried twigs, in dark woods alone
I love you
and by the nest of the mother bird
nervous and angry at the sight of me
I love you
I don't remember anything without love of you
I cannot remember living without drawing breath.

David Ignatow

Yei-ie's Child

I am the child of the Yei-ie.
Turquoise for my body, silver for my soul,
I was united with beauty all around me.
As turquoise and silver, I'm the jewel
    of my brother tribes and worn with pride.
The wilds of the animals are also my brother.
The bears, the deer, and the birds are a part
    of me and I am a part of them.
As brothers, the clouds are our long, sleek hair.
The winds are our pure breath.
As brothers, the rivers are our blood.
The mountains are our own selves.
As brothers, the universe is our home and
    in it we walk.
With beauty in our minds,
With beauty in our hearts, and
With beauty in our steps.
    In beauty we were born.
    In beauty we are living.
    In beauty we will die.
    In beauty we will be finished.

Charles C. Long

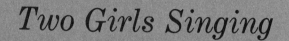

Two Girls Singing

It neither was the words nor yet the tune.
Any tune would have done and any words.
Any listener or no listener at all.

As nightingales in rocks or a child crooning
in its own world of strange awakening
or larks for no reason but themselves.

So on the bus through late November running
by yellow lights tormented, darkness falling,
the two girls sang for miles and miles together

and it wasn't the words or tune. It was the singing.
It was the human sweetness in that yellow,
the unpredicted voices of our kind.

Iain Crichton Smith

The Little Trumpet

All that is left
of the magic of the fair
is this little trumpet
of blue and green tin,
blown by a girl
as she walks, barefoot, through the fields.
But within its forced note
are all the clowns, white ones and red ones,
the band all dressed in gaudy gold,
the merry-go-round, the calliope, the lights.
Just as in the dripping of the gutter
is all the fearfulness of the storm
the beauty of lightning and the rainbow;
and in the damp flickers of a firefly
whose light dissolves on a heather branch
is all the wondrousness of spring.

Corrado Govoni

Translated by Carlo L. Golino

At Quitting Time

At quitting time
a combine clatters unseen behind a hill,
then emerges over the crest,
flowering orange against the sky.
The driver shuts off his engine.
Sweat and dust burn
in his swollen, red-rimmed eyes.
When he climbs off the seat and jumps down,
the field sways beneath him.
He is buried by silence,
lost in it.
Coming down the hill
to where he parked his car in the morning,
he is slowly becoming someone else,
entering another country.
Where he walks,
puffs of dust behind him
turn golden
in slanted sunlight.

Robert Sund

Laying the Dust

What a sweet smell rises
        when you lay the dust—
bucket after bucket of water thrown
on the yellow grass.
                    The water
flashes
each time you
make it leap—
            arching its glittering back.
The sound of
            more water
pouring into the pail
almost quenches my thirst.
Surely when flowers
grow here, they'll not
smell sweeter than this
                wet ground, suddenly black.

Denise Levertov

Evening

The sun horse panting and snorting
Reaches the shores of evening
Kicking his hoofs and flicking red dust
His vermilion mane wet with perspiration
He throws red foam from his mouth

The mellow-colored Evening comes
And places her hand between his pricked ears
Her long fingers
Feel the hot breath from his nostrils
And take off the bridle from his mouth

The restive animal
Tamed and quietened
Walks behind the Evening slowly
And goes into the stable of darkness

Mohan Singh

Translated by Balwant Gargi

VESPER

Now sleep the mountain-summits, sleep the glens,
The peaks, the torrent-beds; all things that creep
On the dark earth lie resting in their dens;
Quiet are the mountain-creatures, quiet the bees,
The monsters hidden in the purple seas;
And birds, the swift of wing,
Sit slumbering.

Alcman of Sparta

Translated by F.L. Lucas

Swan and Shadow

```
                    Dusk
                 Above the
            water hang the
                     loud
                     flies
                     Here
                     O so
                     gray
                     then
                    What        A pale signal will appear
                    When        Soon before its shadow fades
                   Where        Here in this pool of opened eye
                   In us        No Upon us As at the very edges
            of where we take shape in the dark air
              this object bares its image awakening
                ripples of recognition that will
                     brush darkness up into light
even after this bird this hour both drift by atop the perfect sad instant now
                  already passing out of sight
                toward yet-untroubled reflection
             this image bears its object darkening
             into memorial shades Scattered bits of
           light            No of water Or something across
           water               Breaking up No Being regathered
            soon                 Yet by then a swan will have
            gone                     Yes out of mind into what
            vast
            pale
            hush
            of a
           place
            past
     sudden dark as
          if a swan
             sang                    John Hollander
```

The Sky

The sky at night is like a big city
where beasts and men abound,
but never once has anyone
killed a fowl or a goat,
and no bear has ever killed a prey.
There are no accidents; there are no losses.
Everything knows its way.

Ewe origin (Africa)

Translated by Kafu Hoh

Constellations

Night time.
'fore I go to bed,
Grandma say,
Put the water to your head. . .
Shoo
Grandma ole
She say what she want to
And folks say it all true.
What is true. . .
Face all wet
'fore I sleep.
But,
Later on
In my bed
By the window,
I tug the quilt
Tight as the lights out. . .
Shoo
I look 'cross all the roofs I know
Feeling brave,
But the roofs ain't brave.
Farther out I see the bear—
Bear don't scare me—
Dip down
Deep in the blue water
O' grandma's God.
I hear grandma snore, loud
But the bear he don't move.
He stopped there
With the water on his face.
His child near by,
By a million years too. . .
Shoo
What going on that they do
What grandma say.
Everybody know
Grandma ole.

Primus St. John

NIGHT RAIN

I wake with the rain.
It has surprised me.
First, delight,
Then I think of outdoors:
The shovels and rakes I left in the garden
Rusting now in the mist,
The splintering of handles.
I think of car windows open
Tricycles
Canvas cots, trash cans
The hay uncovered
Mildew.

Well, they are out.
And the animals—
The cat, he is gone
The dog is the neighbor's
The horses have a tin roof
If they will stay under it.
And the wild things are there—
Birds, wet in the trees,
Deer in the brush, rabbits in hiding.
The leaves will all be washed
The wild lilacs, the walnuts.

I am sleepy and warm
I dream of the great hornéd owl
Snatching birds like plums out of trees.

Ann Stanford

NUMBERS

I hate and like math.
The letter O
and the number zero sound like
poems about O snowflake. Zero
makes me hungry. It is the emptiest
number in the universe
which is—and is not—round.
The wonder of zero, O snowflake
and the universe
will never be solved.
I want my lunch.

Aliki Barnstone

Author-Title Index